T0025368

BOOKLET THAT EVERY DRIVER IN THE ENTIRE WORLD SHOULD HAVE

DANA M KAY

BOOKLET THAT EVERY DRIVER IN THE ENTIRE WORLD SHOULD HAVE

TATE PUBLISHING

AND ENTERPRISES, LLC

Certificate of Registration
The Certificate issued under the seal of the Copyright Office
In accordance with title 17, United States Code,
Attests that registration has been made for the work identified below. The information on this certificate has been made a part of the Copyright Office records.
Registration Number TXu 1-856-982
Effective date of Registration March 12, 2013

This book is designed to provide accurate and authoritative information with regard to the subject matter covered. This information is given with the understanding that neither the author nor Tate Publishing, LLC is engaged in rendering legal, professional advice. Since the details of your situation are fact dependent, you should additionally seek the services of a competent professional.

The opinions expressed by the author are not necessarily those of Tate Publishing, LLC.

Published by Tate Publishing & Enterprises, LLC
127 E. Trade Center Terrace | Mustang, Oklahoma 73064 USA
1.888.361.9473 | www.tatepublishing.com

Tate Publishing is committed to excellence in the publishing industry. The company reflects the philosophy established by the founders, based on Psalm 68:11,
"The Lord gave the word and great was the company of those who published it."

Published in the United States of America

ISBN: 978-1-63268-207-9
Transportation / Automotive / Driver Education
15.05.22

Acknowledgments

I have few people that deserve acknowledgments for helping me during the writing and giving me moral support when I needed it the most. First of all I want to acknowledge my husband, John A Browne and his daughter Denise Schiltz. She was the one that encouraged me to write this book and give me every possible support. Then comes my own 2 daughters: Nina and her son Thomas and her husband Zbigniew Roczniak they live in Europe but participated in creating this book all the way. My younger daughter Patrycja her son Ney and husband Gerald Bouvier. Their loving support helped me immensely. Here comes my two girlfriends: Joanna Maza and her mother, Danuta Maza they were happy for me when the book was accepted for publishing and can hardly wait to get their copy. I also want to thank my neighbors Patti and Tom Winkler who helped me during signing the contract sending faxes and giving me loving support. Last but not least Ardith and Jim Neidlinger, however Jim didn't believe that I'm going to make it but anyway kept me going. To all people that give me their best wishes and support I have undying gratitude and thankfulness. God bless us ALL.!

Preface

Invisible hand of destiny put the puzzle of my life finally together.

It was my life long dream to publish something that no other came up with up to this time.

I got this material for this booklet by asking universe the questions.

Don't look for the answers, just ask empowering questions and you get the experience, which will be the answer to fulfill your destiny.

It took long time to put everything together; reason for my accident, then overcome fear of driving, then testing my method described in this booklet.

I aspire to publish real book, but I see the urgency of this subject then I decided to publish it as a small pocket booklet first.

English is my second language I have nobody to ask for editing it, my friend that would edit it died 2 years ago of cancer.

In February 2015, I was seventy-three years young, is never too late to accomplish your life purpose.

Please don't judge me too harshly or better don't judge me at all.

I'm putting this booklet in your hands and hoping to change the world.

I'm Aquarius most humanitarian and altruistic and maybe most utopian sign of the zodiac. Also I have a burning desire to make this world better place for all of us.

God bless us all with the wisdom, purposeful lives and safe roads without accidents on the whole world.

—Dana M. Kay

Car Accident Statistics Nationwide for Year 2011

- 6 million – average number of car accidents every year.

- 3 million people are injured every year in car accidents in America.

- Around 2 million drivers experience permanent injuries every year from car accidents.

- 40,000 people lose their lives every year due to major accidents while driving.

- 40% of all deaths caused by car accidents involve alcohol.

- 30% of car accident fatalities are attributed to speeding.

- Reckless driving accounts for 33% of all deaths involving major car accidents.

....

Aug 8, 2008 on my grandson birthday and I was driving to post office heavy car Chrysler Concord. It never happened to me before but this day I felt so relaxed like I have never been before, and I wondered why. I was driving alone on State Road and lost recollection how I get to intersection. Last time I looked at the lights ahead of me I saw them green and was very close to intersection, then is the blank part and in split second when I was already on intersection my eye cut big truck coming on me from the left side I have a time to say only "God" then was this big bang hit and I went into spin couple times my air bag exploded all windows were shattered, my face was profusely bleeding, but I felt at peace, incredible peace and time stand still I was like in different dimension until paramedics arrived. I was hit in the back door on my side with the force that doors on the opposite side fall off from the impact. Car was demolished beyond repair.

Hospital was near by and doctor pulled 22 pieces of glass from my face but left one in my chin that I pulled out myself 4 months later.

I couldn't find the answer why and how it happened. I wasn't tired or sleepy when I was driving. How come I didn't see the truck coming from the left side sooner, was open space around, I didn't speed and I was always responsible driver. Those questions tormented me for more than 4 years, what was the purpose of it? what should I learn from it?

My friend always was telling me that cars are not the toys, but more or less 6000 lbs killing machines, and killing over 40,000 people every year in our country only.

Why is this happening? It's many reasons for accidents: driving under influence of alcohol or drugs, reckless driving, speeding, road rage and carelessness. If you think that driving involve only mental and physical aspects you are very wrong and that is the reason that's so many accidents happen.

We are humans not robots, and we have emotions and if you like it or not we have spiritual parts of us too. This booklet is for every driver in the world. It doesn't matter if you are an atheist, religious or spiritual person.

It's about time that everyone accepts our oneness. We are all connected by our electromagnetic fields, by our mingling auras, by universal collective consciousness and unconsciousness. We are carrying other people's thoughts, emotions and even pain without realizing it. We are all connected and interconnected with each other in so many ways and we don't have any idea about. If you are a parent of the 16 years old, before he/she get driver license give you child this little book to read and to keep it.

If your children start driving with an understanding what is really involved in driving then we are only one or two generations behind save roads and 99% less accidents.

Lets start today with this little book that everyone can afford to buy it. You may be the best driver and you think you don't need any protection except car insurance but let me tell you, if you snort at this idea presented in here then you are an ignorant. Your ignorance wouldn't be bliss when you get into car accident. It's time to tell how I come to those conclusions. Since my accident I lived with constant question WHY? Finally universe provided the answer for me.

....

I lived with a friend that suffered from a cancer and I had to drive sometimes during the night to Emergency at nearby hospital but I was terrified every time I had to drive. My friend died. Then after couple of years I had to move again and drive big moving truck I started to pray and miracle happened, all fear go away and I felt save and secure on the road. From that time everytime I drive now as soon as I enter the car I always say a prayer. I have countless proves that prayer is working like a magic. I feel confident but not careless and my attitude on the road changed dramatically, if I get cut off instead get upset I send the blessing for the driver, when someone honks on me instead show the finger I salute or send the kiss. I saw many times that those reckless drivers that changing lines constantly when I send them blessing they slow down like something or someone cool them down.

When is big traffic on the road I bless all drivers on the road I'm on, all drivers in my city, then in my county, in my country and in the whole world. It gives me such warm feelings of understanding and compassion for all drivers and traffic is dissolved like by the magic very quickly. Did you notice that cars always are driven in clusters and my favor spot to drive is between the clusters, I always thank universe for co-operating with me and giving me my favor space to drive. When the cluster from behind me catch up with me and while they pass me by I send them blessings. At that moment when I do that I feel blessed myself. I explain how it works. If you project something from your heart then this same thing come back to you but multiplied, magnified many times over.

Don't you want have this glorious feeling instead irritation that you are late, that you had an argument with you loved one, that your kids don't behave like you want them to and many other unwanted negative feelings.

Start your driving with payer for safety when you get into your car, then start blessing people on the road and where ever you go to work or just shopping, or taking a trip for pleasure. I guarantee you will have very pleasant day, you will find the best parking spot, you just light up the world around you.

....

The universe gave me another gift. I saw the spiritual aspect of driving like I was in movie theater. It was in Nov 2011 I was in the car with my girlfriend, she was driving, and we were on the Highway and get into stop in traffic because mile ahead was an accident I hear the voice in my head that said one world "watch" I started seeing auras of people in the cars like colors in kaleidoscope and I started to read people emotions mostly was irritation for not moving in gray color but it was mingled with pink of compassion, blue with understanding and green with love and other colors like purple, red and lavender. Then I hear another word in my head that said "pray" I start praying for accident victims and the colors start swirling dissolving the grayness and rushing forward. Traffic start moving, I knew that I had the support of compassionate, understanding and loving people on the road. I knew what I had to do. Now I'm trying to share with you to the best of my ability this spiritual experience. Many awakened people will understand it without any explanation, but the message is for everybody not for only spiritually involved people. Dr David R. Hawkins M.D Ph.D calibrated human emotions on scale from 20–1000 and mapped human consciousness. From 20–200 are negative emotions, low consciousness and low energy levels. Above 200 level people have the power to change any circumstances they find themselves in by applying positive thoughts, emotions and prayers. One person calibrated at 300 level counterbalances 90,000 individuals below 200 level and it grows extra potentially.

One person calibrated at 600 level counterbalances 10 million individuals under 200 level.. This should be motivation for all young readers to achieve the highest levels of consciousness, because it means more successful and happy life.

The prayer is the God given gift and if it comes from the heart it can do a miracles. You don't have to be religious to pray, you can be member of any religion or you can be an atheist and if you love your children you can give them this booklet.

Atheists don't have to say God or God name but invoke something greater than they are and it will do the job. I expect miracles because I already saw it happened for me. I feel as I was chosen to have this accident to know first handed how traumatizing it can be and I was show the way to prevent or minimize accidents on the roads. Now I will tell how I pray. When I get into the car I close my eyes and see parking at destination I'm driving to, then I say;

....

"Dear God hover over me and angels surround me please during my driving and all day long" and ad Thanks or Amen.

If you have passengers say; "Dear God hover over us and angels surround us please during my driving and all day long" ad Thanks or Amen.

....

Then I start the car without fear. I have reverence, courtesy and blessing for all drivers that I'm sending from my heart to every person on the road. That's calibrates me on 300-500 level which counterbalances 90,000-750,000 individuals respectively that they are below 200 level with negative emotions on the road that may cost the trouble for the safe drivers.

Now imagine the area my blessing cover, only little percentage of people drive with pure negative emotions, drunk or under influence of drugs.

Too bad that now I drive once top twice per week and only to nearby food stores. That's is so important that this booklet get to the hands of good people that care for others and be peace makers and accidents dissolvers on the Americans roads and world wide.

Give your small children that you driving with in your car example of this kind of behavior make them assist in your blessings and they eagerly will help you and it became a good habit for their entire life.

I guarantee you will have them become very responsible drivers and adults when they grow up.

You can make up your own prayer, but I think more important are your intentions than what you say, and say it out loud, because the vibration of your voice have more power and if you say it with your children then it will have stronger and better effect on others drivers.

I made this booklet small that you can carry it in your pocket and read it in 15 minutes.

Appeal to the children: all little one boys and girls aspire to make this world of ours better and safer place by achieving higher consciousness and unconditional love to have blissful and joyful life.

For all adults; please show your children the life that you want for them as an example by living it and we all together can change the world.

....

I shared with you my spiritual experiences; I know not all of you will agree that it will make any difference what I said above or how I described it, but that it's not a point. The point is my truth is not everybody truth. Your know your truth is what you feel as good warm feeling around your heart and you feel lighter and you know deep down your heart that is the truth, you know it's right.

If something it's not your truth then you dismiss it quietly and move on or you take a stand against it or call it stupid. The point is we are all different like is no two people with identical finger prints that is not one fact or the truth that we all agree upon it.

Always you will find the people that are on opposite side of your believes and your job is not to convince them to your point of view, but let them be who they are, and you being you, you are saving the world if you don't judge anything and anyone.

Happy people are healthy people with open mind no judgmental and with loving attitude towards life and all people around them.

We all feel sorry for all sick and poor people, but that is what they choose to experience in this lifetime.

You may say I didn't choose any of it that is happening in my life, but believe me you did! Maybe not consciously but you come to this world on your own request for physical life. You were longing for life, you were longing for movement, you were longing for change, and when you were born to this life the first few years you were still connected to the world or dimension you came from. You want proof of that? Take small child that can talk under 6 years old sit him/her on your lap lining towards your chest rub gently his belly in slow circular motion and ask him/her to tell you about the place they come from or of the time when they were big. They are still remember it, they are remember spiritual dimension they come from and they remember past lives.

They still have open the third eye that closes at age 6 or 7 and all thanks or because of our parents or our upbringing.

Don't you saw sometimes little baby under one year old looking up kicking his legs and moving his arms and talking in his language and I can assure you he/she was talking with angels. I hear a story about one little boy that go outside when was dark to see the lights dancing in the trees and his mother goes looking what he was doing in the dark found him sitting quietly with open mouth looking fascinated at the trees and she ask him what he sees there? He said mom don't you see the beautiful lights dancing there in the trees? His mother said cut this nonsense it's not lights in the trees took his hand and walk him home. From that day boy didn't see any more lights in the trees. Here is the best example how we kill the magic in our kids lives.

This same goes for adults with different ideas that not common to ordinary people. People that can't open their minds to all possibilities of life, they can dismiss all they can't comprehend as non existent, but not enough they voice their opinion or judgment. Think for a moment how magical this world would be if we all live in a state of total agreement to our differences.

No calling names, no ridicule, just be and let others be how they are and doing this you can change the world.

We can change the world by cooperating with each other not by competing.

Our world is beautiful abundant place and if we can eliminate the greed and hunger for power over others, then we can live in real paradise.

You may ask what this have to do with driving and accidents, absolutely nothing, but I wanted to show you that we really are "spiritual beings having human experiences" it's the quote invented by Pierre Teilhard de Chardin and used frequently by Dr. Wayne Dyer.

Spiritual aspect of driving is the our oneness on the road how we affecting each other, by our behavior, our attitude, our emotional state and willingness to help and co-operate with each other instead compete or be hostile toward others. If only one person on the each road in the entire world pray and send blessings to rest of the drivers then we can create the world without accidents and save lives lost to accidents.

I should be dead in accident I was in, everyone who saw the car after accident said it was a miracle that I survived and come out of it with only cuts and bruises and I know that God saved me by invoking HIM. My cuts healed without any scars and very quickly, because I was grateful and thankful for my life every day after.

Now I'm giving you in your hands most powerful antidote against all accidents–PRAYER and BLESSINGS.

Then pray and bless and save lives up to 40,000 in United States only.

After submitting my book to the publisher, I had my second minor fender bender accident with a young driver and his passenger because they were playing on their cellphones. Since I didn't use a cellphone, I missed this subject entirely.

. . . .

The word "accident" is excuse for not paying attention to the driving while you are behind the wheel.

Driving and using cell phone at this same time is multitasking and is distracting which can have most tragic consequences in some cases.

Here is appeal to all young drivers who not only talking on the phones during the driving, but texting or playing games that are now available on the cell phones.

If you want to have a clear conscious and not get in any" accident" or kill another driver or even kill the dog on the road "DO NOT USE CELL PHONES " during your driving!

Trust me is not worth it, you will be traumatized emotionally, you incur financial burden of the accident that many of us can't afford to pay at this time or lose your driver license.

Appeal to the parents driving with the children in the car and talking on the cell phones:" DON'T DO IT" it's bad example for your children and give them right to use the phones when they start driving. If you have emergency situation pull over stop the car and then use the cell phone.

I hope my experience make more aware all of you of danger that bring use of cell phones during the driving.

My appeal to all drivers:"DO NOT USE THE CELL PHONES IN THE CARS DURING THE DRIVING"

I hope that when you read it you take it seriously, because if you ignore my warning you may have to pay dire consequences of your ignorance.

It will be ignorance, because you are forewarned now and do not have excuse that you didn't know. "Forewarned is Forearmed " Don't ever forget it!

I'm very spiritual person and I know that is no accidents everything we experience in this lifetime is planed ahead and we have to agree upon it to happen to us consciously or unconsciously, but nothing is written in the stone. God bless us all and keep us save on the roads of the entire world.

I almost missed to put in my booklet the latest cause of many accidents, because when I was writing the book I took statistics from Internet and how you may notice it in beginning of the book is not even a smallest mention about cell phones as a cause of accidents. This was in 2012 now in 2014 is plenty of statistics even there are many movies on Your Tube about use of cell phones as a cost of deadly accidents.

Now we have put this new plague under the microscope and consider pros and cons of it, but first I present you with statistics from Internet:

http://www.edgarsnyder.com/car-accident/cell-phone/cell-phone-statistics.html#teen-cellphone-stats

At any given time during daylight hours, 660,000 drivers in the United States use cell phones. Whether it's texting, taking a phone call, or sending emails, cell phone use is associated with higher rates of dangerous or fatal car crashes. Accidents involving drivers using their cell phones are avoidable but many people put everyone's safety at risk by ignoring laws against distracted driving.

http://www.washingtonpost.com/wp-dyn/content/article/2010/01/12/AR2010011202218.html

Twenty-eight percent of traffic accidents occur when people talk on cell phones or send text messages while driving, according to a study released Tuesday by the National Safety Council.

The vast majority of those crashes, 1.4 million annually, are caused by cell phone conversations, and 200,000 are blamed on text messaging, according to the report from the council, a nonprofit group recognized by congressional charter as a leader on safety.

http://www.nydailynews.com/autos/cell-phone-driving-deaths-underreported-study-article-1.1337271

Driving deaths due to cell phone use underreported: study

A new study reveals that the number of deaths from car crashes in which the driver was talking or texting on a cell phone are underreported. The study reviewed 180 fatal crashes in which cell phone use was a suspected cause and found that only half of the cases were reported with distracted driving as the cause.

http://www.statisticbrain.com/cell-phone-texting-car-accident-statistics/

Cell Phone Texting Car Accident Statistics

Statistic Verification

Source: AAA Foundation, CBS News

Research Date: 6.18.2013

Text messaging, or texting, is the exchange of brief written text messages between two or more mobile phones or fixed or portable devices over a phone network. While the original term was derived from referring to messages sent using the Short Message Service (SMS) originated from Radio Telegraphy, it has since been extended to include messages containing image, video, and sound content (known as MMS messages).

Cell Phone Texting Accident Statistics

Total percentage of people who have sent or received a text message while driving	37%
Total percent of people who text while driving regularly	18%
Total percentage of time spent driving in the wrong lane while texting	10%
Total percentage of people under the age of 18 who admitted to texting while driving	46%
Average amount of time a driver spends not looking at the road while texting	4.6 seconds
Total percentage of respondents who support a ban on text messaging	80%
Total times the amount a truck driver has of getting into an accident while texting opposed to concentrating on driving	23.2

http://www.nsc.org/Pages/NSCestimates16millioncrashes
causedbydriversusingcellphonesandtexting.aspx

National Safety Council Estimates that At Least 1.6 Million Crashes Each Year Involve Drivers Using Cell Phones and Texting

http://www.distraction.gov/content/get-the-facts/facts-and-statistics.html

What Is Distracted Driving?

Distracted driving is any activity that could divert a person's attention away from the primary task of driving. *All* distractions endanger driver, passenger, and bystander safety. These types of distractions include:

- Texting
- Using a cell phone or Smartphone
- Eating and drinking
- Talking to passengers
- Grooming
- Reading, including maps
- Using a navigation system
- Watching a video
- Adjusting a radio, CD player, or MP3 player

The best way to end distracted driving is to educate all Americans about the danger it poses. On this page, you'll find facts and statistics that are powerfully persuasive.

27

If you don't already think distracted driving is a safety problem, please take a moment to learn more. And, as with everything on www.Distraction.gov, please share these facts with others. Together, we can help save lives.

Key Facts and Statistics

- The number of people killed in distraction-affected crashes decreased slightly from 3,360 in 2011 to 3,328 in 2012. An estimated 421,000 people were injured in motor vehicle crashes involving a distracted driver, this was a nine percent increase from the estimated 387,000 people injured in 2011.

- As of December 2012, 171.3 billion text messages were sent in the US (includes PR, the Territories, and Guam) every month. (CTIA)

- 11% of all drivers under the age of 20 involved in fatal crashes were reported as distracted at the time of the crash. This age group has the largest proportion of drivers who were distracted.

- For drivers 15-19 years old involved in fatal crashes, 21 percent of the distracted drivers were distracted by the use of cell phones (NHTSA)

- At any given daylight moment across America, approximately 660,000 drivers are using cell phones

- or manipulating electronic devices while driving, a number that has held steady since 2010. (NOPUS)

- Engaging in visual-manual subtasks (such as reaching for a phone, dialing and texting) associated with the use of hand-held phones and other portable devices increased the risk of getting into a crash by three times. (VTTI)

- Sending or receiving a text takes a driver's eyes from the road for an average of 4.6 seconds, the equivalent-at 55 mph-of driving the length of an entire football field, blind. (VTTI)

- Headset cell phone use is not substantially safer than hand-held use. (VTTI)

- A quarter of teens respond to a text message once or more every time they drive. 20 percent of teens and 10 percent of parents admit that they have extended, multi-message text conversations while driving. (UMTRI)

https://www.youtube.com/watch?v=TY_sdJKblb
https://www.youtube.com/watch?v=nR82z0tzMdc
https://www.youtube.com/watch?v=VX2lqBk-Ovk
https://www.youtube.com/watch?v=u6z0zZS0wFY
https://www.youtube.com/watch?v=gQB5Bl_2GKI

Those five links above can show you blood freezing accidents that you have to consider using cell phones while driving.

The first I address the young people that in age group 16–25, this is the most difficult group to persuade not to use cell phones during the driving, because you youth let you think that you are invincible, that you know better than anyone else that you posses quick reflex and good driving skills. I'm asking you to put all your excuses outside and consider yourself in one of those accidents, but not as victim that end up dead, but the perpetrator that cost this accident. Try to feel as killer that you may become by using cell phone during your driving. Even if you can escape jail time you can't escape your memory that you kill someone, needlessly and irresponsibly because of the cell phone you used while driving. Consider that you will have nightmares and regrets and couldn't enjoy life anymore because your consciousness is not pure or clean anymore. Now if you read this you don't have an excuse, because I'm taking about it to you. This is my warning to you ! Consider yourself forewarned! You probably hear the saying "Forewarned is forearmed" Put outside all your believes about your abilities to drive safely and use the cell phone when you drive. It's multitasking; it's distracting and can be deadly. Now you consider that you are the victim even if you escaped to be dead but got badly injured think about all the pain all the cost all the waist of time to recuperate from it. It may takes moths even years and still you can be an invalid for the rest of your life. Do you want risk yours or someone else life, just by using cell phone?

Now I'm addressing the parents that are drive with children and talking on the cell phones. Please consider that your children learn from you and see you talking on the phone during driving and this automatically became their habit when they reach driving age. I'm daring greatly to be brutal and straight forward about it. If you still driving and using cell phone when you have a child or children in your car after you read this, then I have to tell you are ignorant and arrogant. Ignorance wouldn't be a bliss when you get into accident. You are ignorant because using cell phone during driving is ignorance of your children safety and safety other drivers. You are arrogant because in spite of my warning against use of the cell phones in moving car showing that you don't have any respect toward your own live and lives of others. Imagine you child comes to driving age and perpetuate your habit using cell phone during the driving and get into accident costing it or being victim of it ether way you will live with the guilt and regret for the rest of your life. In the small children you can erase this memory of using cell phone in moving car by immediately quit it, and make a point when you need use the phone pull over and then make phone call. When they ask why you doing it explain that is not safe using phone in moving vehicle, and if you don't do it any more they assume your safe driving as their own. If you don't want to be in shoes the parents that already lost children due to using cell phones, then you have to give them proper example. My life will be worthwhile when even small percentage of people take this message to their hearts and stop using cell phones in moving cars, because otherwise government will be forced to make law against it. Development in communicating technology already costs many lives and when we don't develop understanding between safeties of our lives and convenience of using cell phones during the driving, then no one will be guilty but ourselves for not listen to the reason. Some of the states already passed the law against texting but I'm against using the cell phones in moving cars at all. Don't you think that better be safe than sorry?

May God have a mercy on those who against the reason and better judgment don't quit using cell phones in their cars and keep them safe from harm.

This is my prayer for you and yours.

For comments, you can reach Dana M. Kay through her website, danamkay@tateauthor.com.